STRATEGIC STUDIES INSTITUTE

The Strategic Studies Institute (SSI) is part of the U.S. Army War College and is the strategic-level study agent for issues related to national security and military strategy with emphasis on geostrategic analysis.

The mission of SSI is to use independent analysis to conduct strategic studies that develop policy recommendations on:

- Strategy, planning, and policy for joint and combined employment of military forces;

- Regional strategic appraisals;

- The nature of land warfare;

- Matters affecting the Army's future;

- The concepts, philosophy, and theory of strategy; and,

- Other issues of importance to the leadership of the Army.

Studies produced by civilian and military analysts concern topics having strategic implications for the Army, the Department of Defense, and the larger national security community.

In addition to its studies, SSI publishes special reports on topics of special or immediate interest. These include edited proceedings of conferences and topically oriented roundtables, expanded trip reports, and quick-reaction responses to senior Army leaders.

The Institute provides a valuable analytical capability within the Army to address strategic and other issues in support of Army participation in national security policy formulation.

i

Strategic Studies Institute
and
U.S. Army War College Press

MANEUVERING THE ISLAMIST-SECULARIST
DIVIDE IN THE ARAB WORLD:
HOW THE UNITED STATES CAN PRESERVE
ITS INTERESTS AND VALUES IN AN
INCREASINGLY POLARIZED ENVIRONMENT

Gregory Aftandilian

October 2014

*****

This manuscript was funded by the U.S. Army War College External Research Associates Program. Information on this program is available on our website, *www.StrategicStudies Institute.army.mil*, at the Opportunities tab.

*****

*****

FOREWORD

The Middle East is again in the midst of turmoil. While much of the focus is on the sectarian divide and conflict between Sunni and Shia being played out in several countries and among different groups, an equally important division is occurring between secularists and Islamists in a number of Arab countries. This conflict is particularly acute in the countries of the so-called Arab Spring. The removal of the authoritarian leaders in these countries has led to intense competition between Islamists parties and their secular detractors, and the two sides of this divide have very different visions of where they want their societies to be headed. Islamists initially have an advantage politically because of their history of being a repressed opposition movement, their charitable work among the poor, and their appeal to religion, but secularists, while weak in terms of grass-roots organization, often have powerful institutional allies in these societies, such as the military, judiciary, and trade unions. The secularists also tap into a particular strand that is prevalent in many Arab countries—that religiosity should be a personal decision and not something imposed by the state or a political movement.

In Egypt, where considerable U.S. interests are at stake, the Islamist-secularist divide caused problems for U.S. policymakers, as they were accused of favoring the excesses of either the ruling government or its opponents, depending on to whom they were speaking. With the intense polarization that accompanied this divide, U.S. policies were easily misconstrued as favoring one faction over the other. By the late-spring and summer of 2013, U.S. standing had dropped to a low point.

Mr. Gregory Aftandilian, a Middle East specialist, analyzes this division and explains why it has become so intense. He also examines how the United States has reacted thus far and offers cogent policy recommendations that would help U.S. officials maneuver through this divide while preserving U.S. interests and values. He puts forward specific recommendations dealing with countries in the beginning of the transition period as well as countries already beset by polarization.

The Strategic Studies Institute hopes the findings in this monograph will be of assistance to U.S. policymakers and U.S. Army officers as they deal with the divide facing a number of Arab countries.

DOUGLAS C. LOVELACE, JR.
Director
Strategic Studies Institute and
    U.S. Army War College Press

ABOUT THE AUTHOR

GREGORY AFTANDILIAN, a consultant, scholar, and lecturer, is currently an associate of the Middle East Center at the University of Massachusetts-Lowell, an adjunct faculty member of Boston University and American University, and a Senior Fellow for the Middle East at the Center for National Policy in Washington, DC. He spent over 21 years in government service, most recently on Capitol Hill, where he was foreign policy advisor to Congressman Chris Van Hollen (2007-08), a professional staff member of the Senate Foreign Relations Committee and foreign policy adviser to Senator Paul Sarbanes (2000-04), and foreign policy fellow to the late Senator Edward Kennedy (1999). Prior to these positions, Mr. Aftandilian worked for 13 years as a Middle East analyst at the U.S. Department of State where he was a recipient of the Department's Superior Honor Award for his analyses on Egypt and of the Intelligence Community's Certificate of Distinction. His other government experience includes analytical work for the U.S. Department of Defense and the Library of Congress. Mr. Aftandilian was also a research fellow at the Kennedy School of Government at Harvard University (2006-07) and an International Affairs Fellow at the Council on Foreign Relations in New York (1991-92), where he wrote the book, *Egypt's Bid for Arab Leadership: Implications for U.S. Policy*. He is also the author of the monographs: *Looking Forward: An Integrated Strategy for Supporting Democracy and Human Rights in Egypt* (2009); *Presidential Succession Scenarios and Their Impact on U.S.-Egyptian Strategic Relations* (2011); and *Egypt's New Regime and the Future of the U.S.-Egyptian Strategic Relationship* (2013). He holds a B.A. in history from Dartmouth

College, an M.A. in Middle Eastern studies from the University of Chicago, and an M.Sc. in international relations from the London School of Economics.

SUMMARY

Mr. Gregory Aftandilian examines why the Islamist-secularist divide in such Arab countries as Egypt and Tunisia has become so intense and polarizing and what can be done, from the perspective of U.S. policy, to mitigate such divisions and preserve U.S. interests and values. He demonstrates that having Islamist parties in dominant positions in Arab societies often provokes a backlash from secular elements because the latter see the Islamists as threatening their social freedoms, which leads to unrest. For countries beginning the transitory process from authoritarianism to democracy, Aftandilian recommends that the United States press for a broad governing coalition and a delay in holding elections, similar to what took place in Italy and France toward the end of World War II and which aided the moderate parties. Such practices would allow secular-liberal forces the opportunity to build their political parties and compete with Islamist parties. For Arab countries already facing polarization, the United States should be consistent on human rights, help build up institutions (such as parliaments) as a hedge against authoritarian presidents, and press for inclusionary politics. Aftandilian argues that U.S. assistance should be used as a positive re-enforcer — to reward moderate and inclusionary politics — rather than as a punitive lever (cutting aid) because the latter often provokes a backlash against the United States. In addition, Aftandilian recommends that U.S. Army officers should reinforce to their Arab military counterparts the value and necessity of concentrating on genuine external and internal terrorist threats as opposed to using a coercive internal force that favors exclusionary politics.

MANEUVERING THE ISLAMIST-SECULARIST DIVIDE IN THE ARAB WORLD: HOW THE UNITED STATES CAN PRESERVE ITS INTERESTS AND VALUES IN AN INCREASINGLY POLARIZED ENVIRONMENT

When political analysts and policymakers discuss divisions in the Middle East, they usually refer to the Sunni-Shia split in the region and conflicts, as in Syria, that have exacerbated this sectarian division. However, an equally important division in the region is the Islamist-secularist[1] split, which is most apparent now in Egypt but is also affecting other countries in the Arab world, such as Tunisia, Libya, and even the rebels in the Syrian civil war. This split has led to increased polarization between the Islamist and secular political camps in these countries, often accompanied by zero-sum politics. The challenge for U.S. policymakers is for the United States to preserve and promote its interests and values in these polarized societies, which are increasingly becoming a political minefield, and how to help mitigate such polarization. In some countries, criticism by the United States of one side of the societal divide is seen by that side's supporters as aiding the opposite side. In the case of Egypt, in particular, both the Islamists (particularly the repressed Muslim Brotherhood) and the secularists see the United States as having abetted the excesses of the other side in the tumultuous summer of 2013.

Despite the so-called "Pivot to Asia" that has been talked about in U.S. national security circles, the United States is likely to remain involved in the Middle East for some time to come. Even though new oil and gas discoveries in the United States have made our country depend less on Middle East oil, instability in the region can help drive up prices of these commodities, which would have an adverse effect on the U.S. economy and that of our allies. In addition, while there may be some progress in the P5+1 negotiations with Iran leading to an eventual agreement on the Iranian nuclear issue, many of the Gulf Arab states and Israel are likely to look warily on Iran and would want a substantial U.S. security presence to remain in the region as a counterweight to Tehran. Furthermore, while the leadership core of al-Qaeda has been weakened, there is a now a plethora of al-Qaeda affiliated groups operating in several Arab countries, like Egypt. The United States has vital national security objectives in Egypt, like ensuring the safe and expedited passage of U.S. naval ships through the Suez Canal and overflights for U.S. military aircraft to bring troops to the Gulf region in the event of a crisis.[2]

Hence, the Middle East will continue to occupy the attention of U.S. policymakers and military planners for the foreseeable future despite the refocus on Asia. The United States needs to be able to deal better with the Islamist-secularist division in the area if it hopes to retain its interests there.

WHY HAS THE ISLAMIST-SECULARIST SPLIT BECOME SO VIRULENT AND POLARIZING? AN EXAMINATION OF EGYPT AND TUNISIA

Prior to the Arab Spring of 2011, most countries in this region were ruled by authoritarian leaders who suppressed both Islamist and secular-liberal oppositionists. In so-called republican regimes, power was concentrated in the hands of the president, who was aided by a ruling party that was, in essence, merely

2

an extension of the state apparatus and not an independent institution. Such regimes repressed Islamist parties, even those that eschewed violence, in part because they were afraid that these parties or organizations would challenge the legitimacy of their rule as heads of Muslim states. But these regimes also suppressed secular-liberal parties and dissidents because they challenged the repressive security apparatus and could be seen as alternative political players by Western governments, particularly the United States. Hence, Egyptian President Hosni Mubarak suppressed the Muslim Brotherhood by periodically arresting its activists to keep the organization off-balance and from participating unhindered in the sham of the political process that characterized his rule. He also went after liberal detractors, like Ayman Nour, who criticized the Egyptian leader for the lack of democracy and the repression of dissent, particularly when the United States seemed to look with favor on such oppositionists.[3]

Many citizens who could be classified as secular-liberals often muted their criticism of the regimes, especially when the countries faced challenges from Islamist extremist groups who employed violence. The secular-liberals even lent tacit support at times to the state under the adage that it is better to deal with the devil you know than the devil you do not know. Although they understood and resented the fact that these regimes were ossified and repressive, the secular-liberals at least could be free socially rather than conforming to a very strict interpretation of *sharia* (Islamic law) that the extremists, and even many nonviolent Islamists, seemed to favor. In other words, many saw the secular-orientated authoritarian state as a hedge against a takeover by the Islamists, who were seen as narrow-minded when it came to social norms and practices. The secular-liberals resented the implicit message by the Muslim Brotherhood and other Islamist groups that they were "not Muslim enough." Such secular-liberals believed that neither the state nor a political organization should meddle in their decisions about how devout or not they want to be. In their minds, religiosity should be left to the individual or the family and not be imposed on society. Such sentiments — essentially a separation of mosque from state--were even accepted by many devout Muslim citizens who were wary of Islamist parties.[4]

Additionally, many secular-liberals questioned the pronouncements of the Islamists, even those from the nonviolent and more moderate groups, who claimed that their organizations were committed to democracy. Attempts to form opposition alliances between secular and Islamist groups were often rife with discord, and many secularists were deeply troubled by the writings of some Muslim Brotherhood leaders who seemed to favor second-class status for Christians and women and an Islamic litmus test for laws passed by parliament.[5]

At the same time, the authoritarian regimes, faced with population pressures and increasingly scarce government resources, ceded much of the social welfare space to the Islamists. For example, in Egypt, through their charitable organizations, the Muslim Brotherhood established food banks and health clinics in poor urban and rural areas, often as an ancillary extension of neighborhood mosques. Although occasionally hassled by government security agents, these centers were generally tolerated by the state because they provided essential social services that the state could no longer provide and helped to keep the population quiet.[6] From the Brotherhood's perspective, such activities not only "proved" to the people that the organization cared about their economic plight and fulfilled Muslim obligations of charity to the poor, but also helped maintain the organization's support among a significant segment of the population. In a country rife with corruption, such activities were also seen as altruistic and "clean" by many ordinary citizens, particularly among the semi-educated strata of society, who, along with many middle class liberals, resented the outward displays of wealth by the new class of "crony capitalists" who emerged during the Mubarak era.

The people who initially took to the streets during the revolutions in the Arab world in 2011 were mostly young people of secular-liberal middle-class backgrounds. They were mainly educated and savvy in the ways of social media; they wanted a meaningful and well-paying job, dignity, political freedom, an end to police harassment and brutality, and an accountable government. The Islamist parties initially were hesitant to join the demonstrations because they were not sure of the outcome and did not want to set themselves up for another round of repression by the security services. But eventually some Islamist youth, in defiance of their elders in the organizations, did join their secular counterparts in the demonstrations in the early days because they shared similar goals.[7]

The toppling of several authoritarian leaders in the Arab world was initially greeted by huge displays of national unity, by Muslims and Christians, as well as Islamists and secularists. However, this unity dissipated not long after the revolutions because Islamists and secularists in particular had different visions of their society, and these differences would soon play out in the political arena. Islamist parties seemed to understand their strength from early on in the process, and pushed for elections. They successfully tapped into their networks across the country—particularly in Egypt—and into the perception among many citizens (both in Tunisia and Egypt) that they were a principled opposition party during the dark days of the authoritarian regime who were not tainted by corruption and hence would provide a good alternative to who had ruled them before. The secular–liberal camp was divided and lacked grass-roots appeal. It was mostly congregated in the major urban centers of Cairo and Alexandria and had little outreach to the urban poor, let alone the rural poor. Some were followers of the old liberal parties, like the Wafd, which was formed in the nationalist ferment of the post-World War I years. Others were newly formed "revolutionary" parties that took part in the 2011 revolutions and were good at returning to demonstrations as a tactic but poor at organizing politically, especially in rural areas.[8]

It was not surprising, therefore, that in this context, the Islamist parties did very well in the immediate post-authoritarian elections while the secular-liberal parties did poorly. Egypt's Muslim Brotherhood, for example, won 47 percent of the seats in parliamentary elections in late-2011 and early-2012, while the even more fundamentalist Salafi parties won about 23 percent of the seats. These results compare with secular-liberal parties winning only about 20 percent of the seats overall. In Tunisia, the main Islamist party, En-Nahda, won the largest plurality of votes (37 percent) and the largest plurality of seats (41 percent), while the second largest vote-getter, the secular Congress for the Republic party, won only 8.7 percent of the vote and 13 percent of the seats.[9]

In Egypt, the presidential elections of May and June 2012 produced a Muslim Brotherhood president, Mohammad Morsi, who edged out a secular candidate, Ahmed Shafik, Mubarak's last prime minister and a former head of the air force, in a close race. In the first round of these elections, which saw multiple candidates, Morsi received only 25 percent of the vote, but he was able to win in the second round because of several factors: many Egyptians, disliking both candidates, stayed home, which worked to the advantage of Morsi because the Brotherhood mobilized its supporters to come out and vote; many of the young, secular revolutionaries from 2011 could not stomach a Shafik presidency because of his close association with Mubarak and the old regime and thus threw their support behind Morsi. Morsi cleverly portrayed himself as being a presidential candidate for "all Egyptians," implying he would create an inclusive government. These factors were enough, in the end, to tip the vote in his favor.[10] Egypt's lower house of parliament, which was mentioned earlier and was dominated by the Brotherhood, was disbanded by the courts over a technicality in early-June 2012, but the less powerful Shura, or upper house of parliament, which had a Brotherhood majority, remained intact. Thus, by mid-summer 2012, the Brotherhood controlled both the executive and legislative branches of the Egyptian government.

In Tunisia, En-Nahda ruled in a coalition with two small secular parties, the Congress for the Republic (mentioned earlier) and Ettakatol. As a measure of compromise, the president and speaker of parliament were from the secular parties, while the prime minister was from En-Nahda. But since the power in the new Tunisian political system was titled much more heavily in the direction of parliament than the presidency, En-Nahda, because of its prominent role in the coalition and its control of the premiership, became the dominant political force in the country.[11]

While in power, these leading Islamist parties acted in ways that were seen as either authoritarian (Egypt) or as pursuing policies that were seen as eventually changing the nature of society (Tunisia and Egypt). Moreover, several actions by these Islamist parties seemed to elicit the worst fears of the secularists in those societies. President Morsi, immediately after brokering a truce between Hamas and Israel in November 2012, which received praise from the international community and particularly the United States, issued a decree that said that his presidential decisions would be exempt from judicial review — essentially placing himself above the law. This decree touched off a huge political firestorm in Egypt, leading to violent clashes between the Brotherhood and its liberal detractors in late-2012 and early-2013.[12] In Tunisia, the assassination of two secular leaders — one, Chokri Belaid of the Popular Front who was killed in February 2013, and another, Mohammed Brahmi, a leftist trade union leader who was killed in July 2013 by probable Islamist extremists — caused Tunisia's secular parties to blame En-Nahda for either not cracking down enough on such extremists or creating a permissive environment in which the extremists could operate in the open.[13]

In retrospect, it appears that such policies or the seeming indifference of the Islamist parties to the extremists rekindled secularists' fears of an Islamist takeover of these societies, not just politically but in terms of transforming them into strict and intolerant states whereby personal and cultural freedoms would be jeopardized. Ideological differences between Islamists and liberals are quite profound, as the scholar Shadi Hamid has pointed out. In a recent study, he noted that, while it was campaigning, the Muslim Brotherhood in Egypt espoused a "civilizational project" that, within the framework of democracy:

> offered a spiritual and philosophical alternative to Western liberalism. For Islamists as well as their liberal opponents, it was a question—one that was intensely personal—of how societies would be ordered. Any moral project could be counted on to intrude on private conduct and personal freedoms, on the very choices that citizens made, or didn't make, on a daily basis.[14]

In the same study, he underscored:

> Even what may have seemed, in retrospect, like minor quibbles—over the particular wording of sharia clauses, for example—reflected fundamental divides over boundaries, limits, and purpose of the nation-state. For liberals, certain rights and freedoms are, by definition, non-negotiable. They envision the state as a neutral arbiter. Meanwhile, even those Islamists who have little interest in legislating morality see the state as a promoter of a certain set of religious and moral values, through the soft power of the state machinery, the educational system, and the media. For them, these conservative values are not ideologically driven but represent a self-evident popular consensus around the role of religion in public life. The will of the people, particularly when it coincides with the will of God, takes precedence over any presumed international human-rights norms.[15]

In part because of these sharp differences in views about how society should be governed, Egypt in late-2012 and early-2013 witnessed violent clashes between secularists and Brotherhood supporters. Scores of Brotherhood offices were attacked and torched, even in the city of Ismailiya, where the Brotherhood was founded in 1928.[16] In Tunisia, in 2013, the assassination of two secular leaders, mentioned earlier, set off large street demonstrations against En-Nahda.

Some Islamist leaders like Morsi blamed "remnants of the former regimes" for much of this agitation. While there is an element of truth in this charge, it appears that the Islamist parties miscalculated by not appreciating the depth of anger and fear that the non-Islamist citizenry and political parties had toward the Islamists.[17] In Egypt, this anger eventually gathered steam and support through the Tamarod (rebel) movement—a petition drive to compel Morsi to hold new presidential elections, which was supported by the leading secular parties that formed a coalition called the National Salvation Front. Millions of Egyptians signed the petition, though the exact number is the subject of some dispute, and throngs of citizens gathered in Cairo's Tahrir Square and other venues to demand Morsi's resignation.[18] These demonstrations prompted the Brotherhood to stage counterdemonstrations in other parts of Cairo in support of Morsi. The Egyptian military then entered into the political fray by calling on both sides to compromise for the sake of the country's stability, though it soon became apparent that the military's loyalties were with the anti-Morsi crowds. After Defense Minister Abdel Fatah al-Sissi held a private meeting with Morsi, during which Morsi refused to compromise, the military stepped in and ousted him, placing him under arrest.

It then appointed an interim civilian government under the leadership of Adly Mansour, head of the Supreme Constitutional Court, who became interim president, though al-Sissi clearly was the power behind the scene.[19]

During the course of the next several weeks in Egypt, the military and police forces mounted an aggressive campaign against the Brotherhood, arresting hundreds of its leaders. In mid-August 2013, the Egyptian security forces violently broke up the pro-Morsi protest encampments in Cairo, during which over 500 Brotherhood supporters and some 42 police were killed.[20] Egypt then descended into a very violent period, when scores of Coptic Christian churches and police stations were attacked by Brotherhood supporters, while several hundred more Brotherhood activists were killed by the security forces and thousands more were arrested.[21] In the meantime, Islamist extremist groups emanating from the Sinai Peninsula embarked on a terror campaign against the new regime, the police, and the military from the summer of 2013 to the winter of 2014; at least 300 security personnel were killed by those extremists in either bomb attacks or armed clashes. The new regime lumped the Brotherhood and the Islamist extremists together as a common foe, and in late-December 2013 declared the Brotherhood to be a "terrorist organization."[22]

Facing widespread anger from secularists—particularly from trade unionists and the liberal and leftist intelligentsia, some of whom formed their own "Tamarod campaign"—and seeing what had happened to the Brotherhood in Egypt, En-Nahda decided to compromise. After many weeks of negotiations with secular elements and parties, in September 2013, En-Nahda agreed to relinquish the premiership and its dominant position in the government.[23] A technocratic interim government was appointed in its stead in early-2014, and various elements within the Tunisian polity convened and rewrote the constitution, which has since been deemed to be one of the most progressive constitutions in the Arab world.[24] Elections to a new parliament are expected to take place later in 2014.

Thus, the Islamist-secularist divide has played out very differently in Egypt and Tunisia. Although both societies were and remain deeply split, the divide in Egypt resulted in extensive violence and the incarceration of over 10,000 oppositionists (mostly Brotherhood activists and supporters), whereas the divide in Tunisia has resulted in peaceful political compromise, though with the Islamist party losing its dominant position.

HOW HAS THE UNITED STATES RESPONDED SO FAR TO THE ISLAMIST-SECULARIST DIVIDE?

The Arab Spring of 2011 brought about a new assessment within U.S. policy circles about the U.S. approach to Islamist parties. Although prior to that, the United States did maintain ties with a few Islamist parties in some Arab countries—for example, in post-Saddam Iraq and Morocco—it was reluctant to upset the leaders of other Arab countries, like Mubarak of Egypt and Ben Ali of Tunisia, who made it known that they would view as hostile any relationship between the United States and such parties or organizations. When those regimes were overthrown and the Islamist parties became legal, U.S. policy adjusted accordingly. U.S. policymakers sought to cultivate ties with these parties because they were the best organized within the polity and appeared to be the most popular in several countries. Consequently, in Egypt, especially during the first year after the 2011 revolution, when U.S. officials traveled to Cairo, they would usually visit the Supreme Council of the Armed Forces (SCAF) and the Brotherhood, while bypassing or giving short shrift to the secular-liberal parties.[25] Although the plethora of such secular-liberal parties meant that it would be very difficult logistically to meet each one of them in their own headquarters — U.S. officials often preferred to meet them in a group setting in one location — it gave the impression that the United States was interested only in the military and the Brotherhood, two illiberal organizations, to the detriment of what the other parties believed were the true democratic and liberal forces.[26]

As can be imagined, the U.S. approach did not sit well with most of the secular-liberal parties. It became conventional thinking among the secular-liberal intelligentsia in Egypt that the United States had put all of its eggs in the Muslim Brotherhood's basket, and this feeling was reinforced during the Morsi presidency.[27] The United States was relatively silent when, in late-November 2012, Morsi declared his decrees to be no longer subject to judicial review, because he had just worked with Hamas to broker a truce with Israel after a flare-up occurred between the two belligerents. After praising Morsi for brokering this truce, the United States apparently did not want to upset him by turning on his undemocratic domestic policies, but that policy only fed conspiracy theories in Egypt of U.S.-Brotherhood collusion.

Perhaps more importantly, U.S. officials, at least initially, did not seem to understand how polarizing the Muslim Brotherhood was in Egyptian politics. The fact that Morsi won the presidency did not mean that a majority of Egyptians had adopted the Brotherhood's agenda. He won for the reasons mentioned earlier, and the Brotherhood's true support was probably around 25 percent of the populace.[28] When Morsi issued his controversial November 22, 2012, decree, this latent anti-Brotherhood sentiment came to the fore. When Morsi rushed through a referendum on a constitution that was drafted primarily by his Brotherhood allies the following month, the anger of his substantial number of detractors also burst onto the surface.[29]

Moreover, Morsi also seemed to have underestimated the strength of the secular-liberals in Egyptian society. The fact that the political parties representing this segment of society did poorly at the polls and did not have a mass base obscured the strength and resiliency of this group, which also had allies in the Egyptian judiciary. Hence, by misreading the election results (both of the parliamentary and presidential elections), U.S. policymakers seemed to have concluded that the secular-liberals were an insignificant force. It was not surprising, therefore, that U.S. officials seemed to have concluded that continuing their relationship with the Brotherhood — especially because Morsi hailed from that organization — was the only logical policy.

By the time the United States had a change of heart toward Morsi — stepping up criticism of his repressive domestic policies in early-2013 — it had already lost the support of Egypt's entire secular-liberal intelligentsia.[30] Although the United States was cognizant of this estrangement on the part of the secular-liberals and tried to mend fences with them — in early-March 2013, for example, Secretary of State Kerry stated upon his arrival in Cairo, "I come here on behalf of President

Obama, committed not to any party, not to any one person, not to any specific political point of view."[31] Such comments did little to assuage the concerns of Morsi's many detractors.

That same spring, young, secular activists started the Tamarod (rebel) campaign, which was essentially a petition drive to compel Morsi to hold new presidential elections. The campaign hoped to receive more signatures from Egyptian citizens than the amount of votes Morsi received as a presidential candidate, thereby delegitimizing his presidency. The Tamarod activists were supported by a coalition of secular opposition parties called the National Salvation Front, which was made up of some of the country's leading oppositionists at the time—former Foreign Minister and Arab League Secretary General, Amre Moussa; former International Atomic Energy Agency (IAEA) and chief Mohammad El-Baradei, who was head of the Constitution party; and socialist politician Hamdeen Sabahi.[32]

U.S. policymakers, while recognizing the mounting opposition to Morsi and the Brotherhood, still believed they had no choice but to deal with Morsi, who, despite all of his faults, was the democratically elected president of Egypt. On June 18, 2013, U.S. Ambassador to Egypt Anne Patterson delivered a speech in Cairo in which she tried to dispel notions of a U.S.-Brotherhood conspiracy and explain why the United States maintained relations with Morsi, saying that the United States would work with whoever won elections that met international standards. However, the most controversial aspect of her speech was her indirect criticism of the Tamarod campaign. She expressed skepticism that street protests would produce better results than elections and called on Egyptians to "roll up their sleeves" and work hard to join and build political parties "because there is no other way."[33] A few days later, Patterson met with Khairat al-Shater, not a government official but a Brotherhood leader, in an effort to have him persuade Morsi to reach out to the opposition. Although this message did not make any headway, the mere fact that such a meeting took place fed the secular-liberals' conspiracy theories of a U.S.-Brotherhood alliance.[34] From the standpoint of many within this camp in Egypt, the United States was not a neutral party but a facilitator of Morsi and the Brotherhood's authoritarian policies.[35] Anti-U.S. sentiment, already high, increased among the secular-liberals, and Patterson's image was crudely depicted on placards carried by the anti-Morsi demonstrators who gathered in Tahrir Square and elsewhere.[36]

Thus, by the time that Morsi was overthrown by the Egyptian military on July 3, 2013, with the con-currence of millions of Egyptian citizens, the U.S. standing in Egypt had reached a low point. There was a widespread belief among anti-Brotherhood Egyp-tians that the United States had aided and abetted the Morsi government and thus was complicit in its authoritarian and sometimes repressive policies.[37] The United States tried to steer a middle course after Morsi was overthrown. President Barack Obama, while ac-knowledging the "legitimate grievances of the Egyp-tian people," nonetheless said the United States was "deeply concerned by the decision of the armed forces to remove President Morsi and suspend the constitu-tion."[38] Hoping not to burn its bridges with the Egyp-tian military, however, the United States did not call Morsi's removal a coup because that would have led to an immediate cutoff of U.S. aid under existing U.S. legislation. This middle course, however, satisfied no one in Egypt. The Egyptian military and the secular-liberals were upset that the United States criticized what had happened on July 3, believing it was a genuine revolution that should have been supported by Washington,[39] while the Muslim Brotherhood, seeing the U.S. reluctance to call Morsi's ouster a coup, believed that the United States had given the Egyptian military a "green light" to remove their president.[40]

Subsequent attempts by the United States and the European Union (EU) that summer to bring about reconciliation between the new Egyptian authorities and the Brotherhood failed. Although the United States still refused to call Morsi's ouster a coup, it held up the delivery of F-16 jets to Egypt, in early-August 2013, probably as a lever on the new Egyptian government led behind the scenes by Defense Minister al-Sissi. But even this small slap on the wrist was criticized by al-Sissi as "not the way to treat a patriotic military."[41] When the Egyptian military authorities, against the advice of the United States, violently broke up the pro-Morsi protest encampments in Cairo in mid-August 2013, with much loss of life, President Obama interrupted his vacation to denounce the actions as "deplorable." Obama then decided to suspend the Bright Star joint military exercises with Egypt and added that his administration would review U.S. military aid. In October 2013, the Obama administration decided to suspend most military equipment sales to Egypt, though it continued to provide the more modest economic assistance as well as some counterterrorism aid.[42] The U.S. Congress also exerted its influence on the military assistance issue. While approving the usual $1.3 billion in U.S. military aid in the FY14 Omnibus spending bill, Congress attached conditions on it, such as dividing the aid into two tranches and tying this assistance to Egypt's reaching certain democratic benchmarks that would have to be certified by the Obama administration.[43]

This military aid suspension and the conditionality placed on it led to even more friction in the U.S.-Egyptian bilateral relationship. It did not, moreover, lead to any lessening of the Egyptian government's repression of the Brotherhood (and some liberal detractors of military rule), as some policymakers might have hoped. Although in April 2014, Secretary of State Kerry announced that the United States would resume the delivery of 10 *Apache* helicopters to Egypt because of their importance in counterterrorism operations against al-Qaeda affiliated terrorists in the Sinai, he emphasized that this delivery was related to counterterrorism assistance[44] (which was exempt from congressional conditionality on U.S. aid to Egypt). Kerry, while acknowledging some progress in Egypt, such as the passage of the new constitution, was reluctant to certify that Egypt had met the democratic benchmarks enunciated by Congress—in part because an Egyptian court had just issued hundreds of death sentences against Brotherhood activists and supporters, which several influential members of Congress had criticized. Some members of Congress also were critical of the Egyptian government's arrest of some journalists and some secular activists, who came to criticize the military's rule. Given that these convictions and arrests were seen as egregious violations of human rights, the U.S. State Department also issued condemnations of them.[45]

In Tunisia, the United States was largely spared the wrath it encountered in Egypt. Although a similar (though smaller) Tamarod campaign took place in Tunisia against En-Nahda in the summer of 2013 in the aftermath of the assassination of leftist leader Brahmi, such demonstrations,[46] led in part by trade unions, were not accompanied by an anti-U.S. agenda. This may be explained by the fact that the U.S. role in Tunisia never matched that in Egypt, both in terms of aid and visibility, and Tunisia's closest relationship in the West was with France (its former colonial power), not the United States.

In contrast to the situation in Egypt, which led U.S. policymakers to go through all kinds of political contortions to try to steer a middle course as the military and security forces cracked down hard against the Muslim Brotherhood, U.S. officials heaped praise on Tunisia's political factions for reaching a compromise in 2013 without violence. U.S. officials participated in the inauguration ceremony marking the passage of Tunisia's new constitution in January 2014,[47] and Secretary Kerry flew to Tunis the following month and stated on his arrival:

> I wanted to come here today to confirm on behalf of the American people and President Obama our commitment to stand with Tunisia and the people of Tunisia and to help move down this road to democracy.[48]

He added that Tunisia's new constitution "is grounded in democratic principles, equality, freedom, security, economic opportunity, and the rule of law." It is a constitution, Kerry continued, "that can serve as a model for others in the region and around the world."[49] In April 2014, Tunisia's interim prime minister Mehdi Jomaa, an independent technocrat, was welcomed in the White House by President Obama. Obama said that while some Arab countries have had difficulty in the transition process, "in Tunisia, where it all began, we have seen the kind of progress that I think all of us had been hoping for, although it's been full of challenges."[50] That same month, the United States announced it would provide Tunisia with a $500 million loan guarantee that would make it easier for Tunisia to borrow money abroad; this was the second loan guarantee that the United States provided Tunisia; the first one was given in 2012 for $485 million.[51]

Clearly, the United States was holding up Tunisia as a model for other Arab transition countries to emulate, and was rewarding it with financial support. The underlying message was that the United States favors compromise between Islamists and secularists, and wants such compromises to be settled peacefully. The problem is that the confluence of forces that made peaceful compromise work in Tunisia—a strong middle class, a secularist tradition going back to the days of the French protectorate, a vibrant and secular trade union movement, and a more politically savvy Islamist party that saw the writing on the wall (if it did not compromise it might have faced the same fate as the Muslim Brotherhood in Egypt)—may be, and probably is, absent in other Arab countries.[52] Hence, while it was proper for the United States to praise and reward Tunisia (in contrast to Egypt) for the way it handled its political disputes, U.S. policymakers cannot rely on other "Tunisias" to appear. Instead, it must deal with more complicated and problematic countries that are likely to chart a different path. Nonetheless, there are some lessons that can be drawn from the Tunisian experience that U.S. policymakers can work toward like the value of coalitions. Before countries experience extreme polarization and violence, as we have witnessed in Egypt, where the United States does not have much room to maneuver, the United States can fashion policy prescriptions for what it would like to see in Arab transition countries.

HOW DO U.S. INTERESTS AND VALUES LINE UP WITH POLITICAL FORCES IN THE ARAB TRANSITION COUNTRIES?

The preceding analysis has shown that having Islamists in power either exclusively or in a dominant position tends to be a lightning rod for non-Islamist groups in Arab societies. Whether real or imagined, secularist elements of society see Islamist groups as threatening their way of life, and more specifically, their personal freedoms. The question arises whether the United States has any role to play in this process. In other words, should it simply stand aside and let the politics play out in these societies, or should it try to influence the course of events to seek one outcome over another? Would playing such a role in these societies constitute egregious interference in their internal affairs, or, because of the widespread perception in these societies that the United States is somehow involved in their internal affairs anyway, does it even matter that the United States declares that it has a policy toward Arab transition countries?

In addition, would it make sense for the United States to have two policies on the Islamist-secularist divide, one to be applied before the transition gets under way and the other if and when these societies are polarized and politics become a zero-sum game? This monograph argues that such a two-tier approach is warranted, with the understanding that the United States may not succeed in either case, because it will be the peoples and leaders in these societies who

21

will ultimately choose which path to follow, and they may wish to disregard U.S. advice. Nonetheless, the United States should at least try to develop and carry out a policy of dealing with this divide as opposed to reacting to events on an ad hoc basis.

This monograph also argues that it is in the U.S. interest not to favor a dominant position for Islamist parties in Arab countries for both foreign and domestic policy reasons. Although historically, secular-nationalists in the Arab world (such as Egypt's Gamal Abdel Nasser) have been as much opposed to U.S. foreign policies in the region as have Islamist movements, there can be a mending of fences between such secular nationalist governments if some foreign policy problems can be addressed. For example, Nasser's successor, Anwar Sadat, one of his comrades in the Free Officers organization, which overthrew the Egyptian monarch in 1952, was able to establish close ties to the United States in the 1970s once U.S. policy was committed to the peace process and helped Egypt retrieve the Sinai Peninsula from the Israelis. This is not to say that an Islamist government cannot cooperate with the United States from time to time on some issues, as occurred between Morsi and the United States during the Gaza flare-up in November 2012. But Islamist parties, because they are wedded ideologically to a particular worldview, which sees the West not just as a political opponent but a nefarious power that wants to change the nature of their societies, are particularly loathe to be seen cooperating with the United States and the West in general.[53] It should be remembered that the Muslim Brotherhood's main mission when it was formed in the late-1920s was to counter Western influence in Egypt, believing that much of Egyptian society has forsaken its Islamic roots because of this

Westernization, and the Brotherhood still believes in the Islamization of society.[54] In other words, opposition by Islamists to the West and the United States is not just political, but fundamentally cultural. They can still view the United States as an enemy even after resolving some political issues. By contrast, secularists by and large do not have this deep cultural antipathy toward the United States. For all of his anti-U.S. stances, for example, Nasser admired American society, and was particularly fond of American movies.[55]

On domestic issues, the United States is more in tune with the secular-liberal groups in terms of their values and support for human rights. Although some secular groups in the Arab world believe that the *sharia* has a role to play in the formulation of laws passed by parliament—for example, even the post-Morsi new Egyptian constitution, passed in January 2014, states that the principles of *sharia* are the main source of legislation[56]—secular-liberals generally believe that religiosity should not be forced on society by either the state or a political party, and that political freedoms of press, speech, and assembly are sacrosanct. As of this writing, the conflict between *sharia* and human rights has become problematic in Egypt because, while the new constitution guarantees these rights (including gender equality), the military-backed authorities in Egypt have restricted such freedoms in the interest of stability and "preventing chaos."[57] Nonetheless, with these values and rights enshrined in the new constitution, U.S. officials and secular-liberal activists can hold political leaders accountable to these standards. Moreover, old draconian laws can be done away with by a new parliament that is committed to the application of international norms and rights.

Finally, it is also in the U.S. interest for Arab countries to be stable and not go through violent upheavals on a monthly basis. This means that, while it is not in the U.S. interest (for the reasons mentioned above) to have Islamist parties in a dominant position in these countries because these parties are so polarizing, it is also not in the U.S. interest for these countries under secular rule to practice exclusionary politics in which they shut out nonviolent Islamist parties from participating in the political system. In Tunisia, after En-Nahda agreed to compromise and relinquished power, a secular political leader said that he would not be averse to having En-Nahda in a coalition government with his party after new parliamentary elections are held in the latter part of 2014. After the political turmoil in Tunisia in 2013, this was seen as a statement of reconciliation of sorts.[58] Unfortunately, in Egypt right now, we are witnessing the opposite situation. The Egyptian authorities have designated the Muslim Brotherhood as a terrorist organization, and there appears no chance of reconciliation over the short term.[59] The severe crackdown on the Brotherhood in the summer of 2013 may have driven some elements of the Brotherhood to commit acts of violence, and hence the regime's terrorist labeling of the Brotherhood may have actually become a self-fulfilling prophecy. There are certainly genuine Islamist terrorist groups in Egypt to the right of the Brotherhood that have committed numerous acts of violence against the regime, but the Egyptian government's inclination is to lump all Islamist groups together and say it faces a terrorist threat from them all.[60] This type of exclusionary politics is unlikely to bring stability to Egypt, and even some secular-liberals who are opposed to the Brotherhood understand the potential danger of exclusionary politics.[61] The following historical analogy may be illustrative of what worked in the past in another part of the world in which the United States was deeply involved, and may be of benefit to U.S. policymakers who are seeking optimal outcomes in Arab transition countries.

Post-World War II Strategy in Western Europe as an Analogy.

Although the Arab world and Western Europe represent different cultures, and some observers may resent a comparison of Islamism (using Islam as a political ideology) with Communism, there are lessons that the United States can draw from the past about how new political systems, parties, and elections emerged in post-war Italy and France that have applicability to political transitions in the Arab world.

In Italy, for example, after the liberation of Rome in 1944 but before the end of the war in 1945, various political groups formed the Committee of National Liberation. This council was comprised of the newly formed Christian Democrats, the Communists, Socialists, the Action Party, and the liberals. This coalition lasted until 1947. There were several reasons for this cooperation: 1) the war was still going on in 1944 and in the first half of 1945, and non-fascist Italians wanted to show the outside world that Italians themselves could take charge of their country while fighting the Germans and the remnants of Mussolini's regime in cooperation with the Allies; 2) the Communists were under instructions from Moscow to participate in coalition governments; and 3) the Christian Democrats, as a new party, needed time to develop and did not want to hinder the anti-fascist coalition. The Italian Communist Party, because of its prominent role in the anti-German and anti-Italian fascist resistance, was clearly the up-and-coming party in 1945. By the end of 1945, the Communist party had about 1.76 million members and controlled many sections of Italy.[62] One Communist party cadre from Sesto San Giovanni explained later, "At the time, the party at Sesto was everything. Instead of going to the local government offices, people came to us, at the Rondo, for housing, for jobs, for welfare assistance."[63]

As one of the leading experts on the history of Italian politics has written:

> Both the left-wing parties [the Communists and the Socialists] were convinced that as soon as elections were held, they would emerge as the majority force in the country. They were therefore prepared to make substantial concession to the Christian Democrats and the Liberals to ensure that elections were not unduly delayed. Left-wing ministers behaved with great restraint in order to avoid alienating their Christian Democrat colleagues.[64]

> All of this played straight into [head of the Christian Democratic party] DeGaspari's hands. Sensing the ductility of the left, he gained concessions where he could while still managing to postpone the date of general elections. As Minister of Foreign Affairs, he was in frequent touch with the Allies, who intervened to express their desire for local elections to precede national ones. The reasoning was simple: the longer the 'molten lava of 1945,' to use Lombardi's expression, had time to cool, the more chance the moderates had. DeGaspari threatened a governmental crisis unless his viewpoint was accepted. General elections were finally fixed for the spring of 1946, later than any other country that had been under Nazi occupation.[65]

In these elections held in June 1946, the Christian Democrats emerged as the party with the largest plurality, winning 35.2 percent of the vote. The Communists won 18.9 percent, while the Socialist party won 20.7 percent of the vote. Although the combined vote of the Communists and the Marxist-oriented Socialist party was slightly higher than the Christian Democrats, these two parties could not dominate the coalition government as they had initially hoped. Other developments occurred in subsequent years to further weaken the Marxist left in Italy. In May 1947, DeGasperi, backed by the United States, which had just announced the Marshall Plan for the recovery of Western Europe, felt strong enough to dismiss the Communists and Socialists from his cabinet; a more moderate faction within the Socialist party broke away from the party to form a new party; and Moscow gave instructions to Western European Communist parties to no longer participate in coalition governments. When new elections were held in Italy in April 1948, the Christian Democrats scored even more gains, winning 48.5 percent of the vote, while the combined Communist and left-wing Socialist parties won 30.1 percent of the vote.[66]

In France, the three main anti-collaborationist parties — Communists, the Socialists, and France's equivalent of the Christian Democrats, called the Popular Republican Movement — became part of a coalition government formed after Paris was liberated in August 1944, and was under the leadership of General Charles DeGaulle of the Free French Forces until 1946. This government was called "The Provisional Government of the French Republic," and it governed France until 1947, similar to what had occurred in Italy. If elections had been held immediately after the war, there was a good chance that the Communists would have emerged as the dominant political party because of their prominent role in the resistance.[67] Instead, elections were put off until the non-Communist forces were in a better position to contest the elections.

The lesson that can be drawn from these experiences is that Italy and France were in a state of deep political turmoil toward the end of World War II. The old regimes—the collaborationist Vichy government and Mussolini's fascist government—were discredited, and the anti-fascist groups were jockeying for position. They settled on coalition governments in 1944—with support from outside powers—as the best way to bring stability and redemption to their countries. The moderate parties realized that a rush to elections would aid the Communists, because they were the best organized of the resistance groups. Hence, national elections for parliament were delayed by the moderate parties in order for them to build up their national followings. So, when national elections were held in 1946, the Communists were not in a position to dominate the political scene. Outside powers also contributed to this process. Both the United States and the Soviet Union aided the non-Communists and the Communists, respectively, but the non-Communists were able to prevail.[68] Although the Communists continued to participate in the parliamentary systems in Italy and France, and were able to retain a significant following in subsequent years—even winning control of some municipalities—they were never in a position to dominate the national politics of either country completely.

The lessons that can be drawn from these experiences are: 1) political coalitions from a transitional country's political factions can be a stabilizing force in the aftermath of the fall of a discredited regime; 2) delaying elections can give moderate parties a chance

to develop and level the political playing field; 3) inclusionary politics—allowing all political factions,
including more radical elements, to participate in
elections—can be a stabilizing factor; and, 4) outside
powers can play a positive role by working with their
ideological allies in support of coalition politics.

Although in 1947 the Communists were excluded
from government in both Italy and France, non-Communists did not make them illegal. If they had done
so, it is likely that Italy and France would have experienced more instability in the post-war period, since the
Communists were influential in the labor unions and
among the intellectual classes. Forcing the Communists underground may have led to act of subversion
and sabotage, which would have caused numerous
problems in these societies and hindered the development of a Western security umbrella under U.S. leadership. Although at the time, the United States was
not pleased that the French and Italian Communist
parties, which were pro-Moscow, remained legal enti-
ties in these countries, especially at the time when the
Cold War had solidified. In retrospect, keeping these
parties in the political system (though not in government) proved to be a wise policy.

RECOMMENDATIONS FOR U.S. POLICY

Dealing with Countries Immediately after the Overthrow or Resignation of the Autocrat.

This monograph posits seven recommendations:

1. As the examples of Italy and France in the immediate post-war years have shown (as has Tunisia
post-2013), it is best for achieving stability and lessening the chances of polarization for Arab transition

countries to adopt coalition governments immediately after the fall of a discredited autocratic leader. The United States should encourage the remaining institutions of the old regimes, such as the military and the judiciary, which perhaps have not been overly tainted by repression, and the countries' political forces to come up with a suitable formula of party representation in these new governments. Given how polarizing Islamist parties are among secular groups, it should be emphasized to the power brokers that while Islamists should have a significant presence in these coalitions, they should not have a majority position in them. If a visible U.S. role in this endeavor would be seen as counterproductive by the political players, the United States should work together with its regional allies behind the scenes, with the political factions over which the United States and its allies have some influence. This combination of inside and outside influence may succeed in bringing about a relatively stable and representative coalition that will be accepted by the populace. As alluded to earlier, the post-war coalition governments in Italy and France had a certain amount of legitimacy because they were made up of anti-fascist forces. But the United States and the Soviet Union also played a role in supporting their allies in these coalitions and encouraging them, at least initially, to cooperate with the other parties in the coalition.

2. The United States should promote that the coalition government be given both executive and legislative powers. Decisions should be reached by consensus, which will lead to a buy-in by all of the political factions. These political forces will thus see the coalition government as "their" government, because they will have an important role in the decisionmaking process. To avoid the appearance of domination

by one faction over another, the head of the coalition government should be rotated every 4 months or so. The head of government, however, is merely a ceremonial position, and real power rests with the actual coalition.

3. The United States should encourage the coalition government to enact reforms, immediately, that show a clean break from the old regime. Emergency laws should be abolished, and freedom of speech, press, and assembly should be guaranteed. The coalition government should also emphasize rule of law and end the practice of crony capitalism to show the populace that the political parties are in favor of a level playing field for all citizens. In this vein, the internal security services should be purged of those who committed egregious human rights violations, and a representative body should be chosen by the governing coalition to run the security services.

4. The governing coalition should pick a group of jurists and nonjurists, representing the political factions in the coalition, to write a new constitution that guarantees the freedoms mentioned earlier. Undoubtedly, there will be intense discussions about the role of *sharia* in legislation, but Islamist and secularists, because they are part of the ruling coalition, may be more inclined to compromise with each other than if they were not in the same government. After the drafting of the constitution, the document should be put before the people in a national referendum. The United States should speak out about the need for the constitution to guarantee universal freedoms, but it should avoid commenting on *sharia,* because that would touch a raw nerve and is likely to be counterproductive.[69]

5. The United States should privately encourage the delay of presidential and parliamentary elections for at least 3 years. It would find the most receptivity for this delay among the secular parties, which would be starting out with a disadvantage politically and would want the time to build their parties, develop a coherent ideology and party platform, and organize outside of the main cities. The United States is likely to find the most resistance to the delay from Islamist parties, which would want elections sooner rather than later to take advantage of their grass-roots appeal.[70] As long as the ruling coalition government retains a non-Islamist majority, the secular forces should be able to put off Islamist calls for early elections. If the governing coalition does enact political and economic reforms, the populace might be content in seeing the coalition government continue for this 3-year period and not clamor for elections. Moreover, a relatively long period for a coalition government would work to equalize the political parties in the eyes of the populace. Secular parties that were not well known prior to the revolution or ones that had been formed at the start of the revolution would now be seen as on equal footing as the Islamist parties, which presumably had been more well known to the populace.

6. The United States should encourage American and European nongovernmental organizations (NGOs) involved in democracy promotion to assist political parties of all ideological persuasions (Islamist and secularist) in these countries to develop effective political party strategies, such as messaging, campaigning, and recruitment. If particular Arab countries reject these NGOs as "interfering in their countries' internal affairs,"[71] the United States should weigh in with the ruling coalition to underscore the fact that

such efforts benefit all parties. If these U.S. appeals do not work, the United States should encourage the political parties to send some of their cadres to the United States for training by these NGOs.

7. As in the case now with Tunisia, the United States should reward the governing coalition politically and economically. The United States should praise the development of a progressive constitution and its passage by the public, the settlement of disputes peacefully through coalition politics, and the enactment of political and economic reforms. The U.S. administration can also encourage the U.S. Congress to provide loan guarantees and bilateral direct aid to the country, which will help it deal with pressing problems like infrastructure and unemployment. All of these policies will put the governing coalition in a good light. By the time elections are held, the secular parties will be held in as high esteem as the Islamist party, and chances are they will do well in the electoral contests because they will be seen as responsible and working for the welfare of the people. They will no longer be seen as merely debating clubs of urban intellectuals. Hence, they would stand a good chance of remaining a part of, and even becoming a dominant force in, a new ruling coalition. If the secularists do come out on top after the elections, the United States should use its influence with them not to turn against the Islamists and to allow the Islamists to continue to have a stake in the new political system by participating in future elections.

Dealing with Countries that are Already Highly Polarized in Which Politics Is a Zero-Sum Game.

The most difficult scenario for U.S. policymakers is the one Egypt experienced during the Morsi presidency (2012-13) and is currently experiencing under military/secular rule (2013-14), when exclusionary politics is the name of the game. The winning side believes that the losing side is not only its opponent, but its enemy, which needs to be suppressed. How can the United States maneuver through this sharp and exclusionary divide and still maintain its interests and values?

1. The United States should be consistent on human rights issues, no matter which side is committing the abuses. As mentioned earlier, one of the main reasons the U.S. standing fell to a low point in Egypt, particularly among secular elements, was because the United States failed to criticize Morsi's November 22, 2012, decree that set him above the law. U.S. quiescence was interpreted as U.S. support for Morsi's policies, while conspiracy theories abounded about some type of secret, back room deal between the United States and the Brotherhood. Although the United States was grateful to Morsi for helping to broker the Hamas-Israel truce just days earlier, foreign policy cooperation should not trump an egregious act like the November 22 decree. In addition, when violence is committed by both sides of the divide, the United States should acknowledge this fact as well. For example, it was proper for U.S. officials to condemn the mid-August 2013 crackdown on pro-Morsi demonstrators in which more than 500 died in a single day,[72] but U.S. officials should also have condemned the killing of 42 policemen on that day as well. Granted, there was a large difference in

the numbers of those killed, but some of the pro-Morsi protestors did have arms and used them against the security forces, so at least some of the pro-Morsi demonstrators were not innocent victims.

2. The United States also needs to be consistent in advocating inclusionary politics. When Morsi was in power, it appears that the United States did not press Morsi or the Muslim Brotherhood to bring secular oppositionists into the government until very late in the game, mid-June 2013,[73] only a couple of weeks before Morsi was overthrown. Whether Morsi would have listened to the United States earlier remains an open question. Even if he would not have done so, at least the effort by the United States to push for an inclusionary outcome may have lessened the virulent anti-U.S. sentiment that surfaced in June and July 2013. After Morsi was ousted by the Egyptian military, U.S. and EU diplomats did try to convince Defense Minister al-Sissi and the interim civilian government to not crack down violently on the Morsi supporters and to reach some type of political arrangement with them, but to no avail.[74]

3. The United States should understand that Egypt (and countries that might be in a similar situation one day) is still undergoing a revolutionary period. Historically, revolutions go through different phases, and legalisms are often their first casualty. For example, Mubarak's ouster by the Egyptian military in February 2011 — with power transferring to the SCAF — was technically an illegal act. Under the then-existing Egyptian constitution, power should have been transferred to the speaker of parliament, who would rule for 60 days, followed by new elections for president. But in the heyday of revolutionary euphoria, no one questioned this power transfer, including the United

States, which was pleased that Mubarak had finally stepped down and a pro-U.S. military would rule in his place until elections for parliament and president would be held. In June 2013, as Egypt was in the midst of arguably a second revolution—this time against Morsi—the U.S. response was legalistic. Impending street protests were criticized by U.S. officials; instead, the message was to work for political parties.[75] In a normal situation, this might have been sound advice, but by June 2013, with millions of Egyptians taking to the streets to demand Morsi's resignation, Egypt was in the midst of additional revolutionary upheaval. In such a situation, U.S. officials should have sided with the demonstrators because they represented the majority of the populace. Even though Morsi had been elected democratically, he acted in an authoritarian manner; with the United States calling on Egyptians to stick with Morsi for another 3 years, this message was viewed in Egypt as a policy of having the populace to continue to suffer under authoritarian and incompetent rule.

4. U.S. officials should also understand that in a highly polarized political environment, it is impossible to please both sides. The United States can either downgrade relations and cut off assistance to the winning side to show its dissatisfaction with the winning side's repressive actions or continue its relations with the winning side in the hope that the leverage that comes with such a relationship can be used to decrease the suppression of the losing side. Either way, the idea is to make the winning side less repressive. In the case of some countries that are very prideful of their history, like Egypt, maintaining a working relationship with the regime is usually preferable to cutting off aid because the latter policy will cause a nationalist backlash and ultimately hinder U.S. leverage.[76]

5. In a highly polarized environment, the president of the transition country is usually the one who is the most polarizing figure, as he represents the best or worst of a particular ideology, depending on one's point of view. Hence, it is important for outside countries like the United States to work with parliaments as a check on the excesses of a president. Prior to the Arab Spring, most parliaments in the Arab world were merely mouthpieces of the ruling regime, but post-Arab Spring, parliaments have become more diverse and more independent of the presidency. Moreover, the new constitutions that have emerged and will emerge in Arab transition countries also tend to give more power to parliaments than they had in the past. The United States can also increase funding for its Visitors Program, which brings foreign legislators to this country as a way of persuading them of the benefits of political inclusivity.

Additionally, U.S. officials should encourage the new regime to live up to the liberal clauses in its new constitution, which was substantially rewritten in late-2013 and passed by public referendum in early-2014. Except for the clauses that give the military and the police wide autonomy, the constitution is a progressive document in which liberal freedoms (of speech, the press, and assembly) are protected.[77] It should be the duty of the new Egyptian parliament that will likely be elected in early 2015 to see to it that laws are in conformity to the constitution. If they are not, they should be removed. For example, there are still laws on the books that state a citizen can be arrested for "defaming Egypt." Such a law can be so broadly interpreted that it can easily be used to stifle political dissent. The United States can also use the advent of parliamentary elections to push for as much inclusivity as possible. Although there is little to no chance that the Brotherhood's political arm, the Freedom and Justice party, will be allowed to run in these elections--and U.S. advocacy on this party's behalf will likely backfire--the United States can and should push for as much political inclusivity as possible. This means allowing non-Brotherhood Islamists like the various Salafi parties to participate in the elections so that these elections are not simply a contest among secularists. Over time, once the new parliament is ensconced and the terrorist threat subsides, the government may be more willing to countenance even more inclusivity.

6. In a society under secular rule that is facing a genuine terrorist threat from Islamist militants, like Egypt today, it is unlikely that the United States will be able to convince the authorities that the designation of the Muslim Brotherhood as a "terrorist organization" is both wrong and counterproductive until the terrorist threat is brought under control. As long as terrorist acts are taking place in the country, the authorities will tend to lump all Islamist groups together. Given such strong sentiments, U.S. policymakers must understand that they cannot realistically change the Egyptian government's attitude and policies toward the Brotherhood. Hence, the United States and Egypt, at least over the short term, will have to "agree to disagree" on the Brotherhood. What the United States can do (in conjunction with the EU) is to criticize the Egyptian government when it undertakes egregious human rights violations (such as the quick trials in the spring of 2014 in which hundreds of Brotherhood activists and supporters were given the death penalty), the arrests of journalists for simply doing their job of reporting on opposition activities, and the arrests of young activists for demonstrating

in the streets against the military. Egypt's new regime wants to gain international legitimacy, and, by withholding full legitimacy through the condemnation of such arrests, the United States and the EU can hold the regime to a certain standard.

7. U.S. economic assistance, in a highly polarized environment, should be geared to a high-visibility project that would be seen as benefiting the people over the regime. In this way, the United States can help enhance its image in the country and mitigate the suspicions that the United States favors one side over another in the societal divide.

8. During sharp Islamist-secularist polarization, which is usually accompanied by human rights abuses, the United States should review its military aid to that country to ensure that no U.S. military items are being used for the suppression of internal dissent. If U.S. military items have been found to be used for this purpose, the United States should discontinue any further deliveries of such items and should warn the authorities that continued use of them for such purposes would adversely affect future aid.

9. In general, however, U.S. military aid to countries undergoing polarization should not be cut, because doing so would lessen U.S. leverage either with the regime in power or with that country's military establishment. In particular, if a country is facing an Islamist terrorist threat during heightened polarization, cutting military aid — especially aid that can be used for counterterrorism purposes — can work against U.S. interests, because it will embolden the terrorist groups and give the perception, especially among secularists in the society, that the United States is somehow secretly in league with the Islamists to take over the country.

RECOMMENDATIONS FOR THE U.S. ARMY

The following suggestions for the U.S. Army will preserve and enhance the bilateral security relationship between the United States and Arab transition countries facing political polarization, such as Egypt.

Background.

Many of the countries in the Arab world, including those going through transitions, have had long security relationships with the United States. Such relationships have often involved the sale of U.S. military hardware to the military establishments of these countries (especially to their armies, which represent the largest segment of their armed forces), joint military exercises, the sharing of intelligence for counterterrorism purposes, and, increasingly, help with counterterrorism operations.

Within the Islamist-secularist divide, the military establishments of these countries are usually on the side of the secularists, because they have long seen the Islamists not only as a threat, but as having loyalties outside of the nation-state.[78] Hence, it has been a long-held view of these military establishments that Islamists should not be allowed to join the officer corps, and one of the main tasks of military intelligence in these countries has been to weed out those officers who were suspected of having been members or supporters of Islamist organization like the Muslim Brotherhood and even more radical Islamist groups. During his presidency, Morsi tried to change this prohibition, and pressed the military to include some young Brotherhood members into the military academies.[79] It is likely that this action was one of the reasons Morsi's relations with al-Sissi, whom he had picked to be Defense Minister in August 2012, soured over time.

U.S. Army officers should understand, however, that the opposition of many Arab military establishments to Islamist groups like the Muslim Brotherhood does not mean that the officer corps in these countries is not religious. In fact, many career officers, including al-Sissi, are believed to be quite devout.[80] Many of the wives of Egyptian military officers wear the hijab (the conservative head cover), and most of these officers observe *Ramadan* (the Islamic holy month of fasting). They differentiate between personal religiosity, which they support, and the use of religion for political purposes, which they oppose.

Recommendations.

1. During a period of intense polarization between Islamists and secularists, Arab military officers may lecture their U.S. army counterparts about the "threat" posed by Islamist groups like the Muslim Brotherhood and express sentiments to the effect that the U.S. political authorities are "naïve" in believing the Muslim Brotherhood is a nonviolent group. Because this is a complicated issue and the United States does not agree with the Egyptian and other Arab governments like those of Saudi Arabia and the United Arab Emirates that the Brotherhood is a terrorist organization, it would be best that U.S. Army officers stay clear of such discussions with their Egyptian and other Arab military counterparts as much as possible.

2. Instead, U.S. Army officers should try to focus their discussions with their Arab military counterparts on actual terrorist threats, such as al-Qaeda affiliated

groups that are operating in the Sinai Peninsula, like Ansar Bayt al-Maqdis, which have not only attacked Egyptian military and police units, but foreign tourists as well. Such groups have also attacked government officials and installations in Cairo and other more populated areas of Egypt.

3. Helping Egypt and other Arab countries deal with their actual terrorist threats would not only mitigate Islamist-secularist divisions in these countries but boost the U.S. standing there. It would help to focus the military in these countries on the real terrorist threat, not on nonviolent Islamist groups, and this renewed focus might work to ease up the repression of the latter. Moreover, by helping to focus the Egyptian military on operations in the Sinai, U.S. Army officers would help restore and refurbish the Egyptian military's reputation of protecting the nation from foreign threats and foreign-linked enemies, as opposed to playing a divisive role in domestic politics.

4. The more the U.S. Army can give advice, logistical support, and military equipment to help the Egyptian military put down the terrorist threat in the Sinai, the more the Egyptian people will see the United States as playing a helping hand in bringing about domestic stability. This stability will make tourism rebound (increasing jobs and revenue) and attract more foreign investment into the country. Pacification of the Sinai is thus extremely important on many levels, and the U.S. Army (including its special forces) is best equipped to offer this type of assistance.

5. In addition, because of the knowledge gained by the U.S. Army in counterterrorism operations in Iraq and Afghanistan, it can bring to bear the lessons learned in those conflicts to the Egyptian Sinai context, and against Islamist extremists operating in Tunisia and Libya. Furthermore, U.S. Army officers can

also warn their Egyptian counterparts, for example, about counterterrorism policies that can be counterproductive. These include punishing a whole Bedouin village—and demolishing homes there—in the Sinai, because one or two of this village's youth are believed to have aided the terrorists. Such practices by some Egyptian Army units, which have come to light in the press, can create more enemies than they intended.[81]

6. Although some Egyptian and other Arab military officers, for nationalistic reasons, may resent such advice from their U.S. Army counterparts, their ultimate goal is to end the terrorist threat emanating from the Sinai (in the case of Egypt) and other troublesome regions in their countries, and they may come around and accept this advice. In this regard, the U.S. Army should favor increasing the number of Egyptian military officers coming to the United States for training at U.S. professional military educational institutes. Part of this training should involve effective ways to conduct counterterrorism operations, and another part should include the benefits of civilian control over the military and the military's respect for human rights. By helping the Egyptian military put down the terrorist threat in the Sinai, having it return to its proper role of defending the nation against external threats, and lessening its involvement in domestic affairs, the United States will not only help mitigate the polarization in Egypt and similar societies but rebuild the bilateral security relationship that has frayed since the ouster of Morsi in July 2013.

ENDNOTES

1. I use the terms "secular" and "securlarist" in this monograph because they are commonly understood in the West to refer to individuals who favor the separation of religion from politics.

However, in the Arab world, many secularists prefer not to use these terms, because some Islamists have wrongly and unfairly equated secularism with atheism. Hence, many secularists in the region use the phrase "supporter of a civil state" to describe themselves. For purposes of this monograph, I am using the terms "secular" and "secularist" for reasons of brevity.

2. Gregory L. Aftandilian, "Looking Forward: An Integrated Strategy for Supporting Democracy and Human Rights in Egypt," Project on Middle East Democracy, May 2009, pp. 6-8.

3. Report to the Committee on International Relations, House of Representatives, "Security Assistance: State and DOD Need to Assess How the Foreign Military Financing Program for Egypt Achieves U.S. Foreign Policy and Security Goals," Washington, DC: U.S. Government Accountability Office (GAO), April 2006, p. 17.

4. Personal interviews with Egyptian interlocutors, March 2013. See also Augustus Richard Norton, "The Return of Egypt's Deep State," *Current History*, December 2013, pp. 340-341.

5. Amr Hamzawy, Marina Ottaway, and Nathan Brown, "What Islamists Need to be Clear About: The Case of the Egyptian Muslim Brotherhood," *Policy Outlook*, Washington, DC: Carnegie Endowment for International Peace, February 2007, pp. 6-8.

6. For the type of social-welfare work that the Brotherhood has been engaged in, see Denis Sullivan and Sana Abed-Kotb, *Islam in Contemporary Egypt*, Boulder, CO: Lynne Rienner Publishers, 1999, pp. 26-35.

7. Carrie Rosefsky Wickham, *The Muslim Brotherhood: Evolution of an Islamist Movement*, Princeton, NJ: Princeton University Press, 2013, pp. 160-162.

8. Steven A. Cook, *The Struggle for Egypt: From Nasser to Tahrir Square*, New York: Oxford University Press, 2013, p. 313. See also Norton, p. 339.

9. Shadi Hamid, "The Future of Democracy in the Middle East: Islamist and Illiberal," *The Atlantic*, May 6, 2014, p. 6, avail-

able from *www.theatlantic.com/international/archive/2014/05/democ-racys-future-in-the-middle-east-islamist-and-illiberal/361791/.*

10. Cook, p. 322; Norton, p. 340.

11. Anouar Boukhars, "In the Crossfire: Islamists' Travails in Tunisia," Washington, DC: Carnegie Endowment for International Peace, Paper, January 27, 2014, pp. 5-6.

12. Maggie Michael and Aua Batrawy, "Egypt Clashes Erupt After Morsi's Power Grab," *The Huffington Post*, November 23, 2012, available from *www.huffingtonpost.com/2012/11/23/egypt-clashes_n_2177120.html.*

13. Peter Beaumont, "Tunisia: Killing of Leftist Leader Brings Secularists onto the Streets," *The Guardian*, July 25, 2013.

14. Hamid, "The Future of Democracy in the Middle East," p. 6.

15. *Ibid.,* p. 5.

16. Tom Perry, "Brotherhood Office Torched in Egypt's Ismailia," *Reuters*, December 5, 2012, available from *www. reuters.com/article/2012/12/05/us-egypt-politics-ismailia-idUSBRE8B41AC20121205.*

17. "Morsi Says 'Counter-revolution' is Obstructing Egypt's Development," *ahramonline*, January 24, 2013.

18. Hamza Hendawi, "Egypt Protests: Thousands Gather at Tahrir Square to Demand Morsi's Ouster," *The Star*, June 30, 2013, available from *www.thestar.com/news/world/2013/06/30/egypt_pro-tests_thousands_gather_at_tahrir_square_to_demand_morsis_ouster. html.* On the controversy over the number of signatures gathered by the Tamarod activists, see Norton, p. 342.

19. David Kirkpatrick and Alan Cowell, "Muslim Brother-hood's Leaders Seized in Egypt," *The Boston Globe*, July 5, 2013.

20. Liz Sly and Sharif al-Hourani, "Egypt Authorizes Use of Live Ammunition against Pro-Morsi Protestors, *The Washington Post*, August 15, 2013.

21. Martin Chulov, "Egypt's Coptic Christians Report Fresh Attack on Churches," *The Guardian*, August 15, 2013, available from *www.theguardian.com/world/2013/aug/15/egypt-coptic-christians-attacks-churches*.

22. Erin Cunningham, "Egypt's Military-Backed Government Declares Muslim Brotherhood a Terrorist Organization," *The Washington Post*, December 26, 2013.

23. "Tunisia Coalition Government Agrees to Resign," *Al Jazeera*, September 28, 2013.

24. David Ignatius, "In Tunisia, Hope Springs," *The Washington Post*, January 26, 2014.

25. Comments from the Carnegie Endowment for International Peace seminar, "A Discussion with Amr Hamzawy," Washington, DC, May 4, 2012. Hamzawy is the president and founder of the Egyptian Freedom Party, one of Egypt's liberal parties.

26. Abdel Rahman Youssef, "The Muslim Brotherhood and the U.S. Pragmatic Partners," *Al Akbar* in English, March 9, 2013.

27. *Ibid.* See also Shadi Hamid, "It Ain't Just a River in Egypt," *Foreign Policy*, July 30, 2012.

28. This was the percentage that Morsi received in the first round of presidential elections. Saad Eddin Ibrahim, a prominent Egyptian intellectual and head of the Ibn Khaldun Center for Development Studies, stated at various Washington think tank seminars over the past decade that the Brotherhood probably has the support of about the same percentage of Egyptians — 25. Personal observations.

29. Dan Murphy, "New Constitution Divides Egypt as Economy Falters," *The Christian Science Monitor*, December 28, 2012, available from *www.csmonitor.com/World/Security-Watch/Back channels/2012/1228/New-Constitution-divides-Egypt-as-economy-falters*.

30. See, for example, the open letter to President Obama from a prominent Egyptian human rights activist. Baheiddin Hassan, "Open letter to President Obama," *Al-Ahram Weekly*, February 6, 2013, available from *weekly.ahram.org.eg/News/1328/21/Open-letter-to-President-Obama.aspx*.

31. Ann Gearan, "Kerry Pushes Egypt on Economy; Opposition Figures Keep Distance," *The Washington Post*, March 3, 2013.

32. "'Rebel' Egyptian Movement Defies Morsi Through Petitions," *Al-Monitor*, May 17, 2013, available from *www.al-monitor.com/pulse/originals/2013/05/rebel-movement-egypt-early-elections.html#*.

33. "Ambassador Anne W. Patterson's Speech at the Ibn Khaldun Center for Development Studies," June 18, 2013, available from *egypt.usembassy.gov/pr061813a.html*.

34. Michele Dunne, "With Morsi's Ouster, Time for a New US Policy Toward Egypt," *The Washington Post*, July 4, 2013.

35. Abigail Hauslaohner, "Egyptian Group Accuses US of Keeping Morsi in Power," *The Washington Post*, June 30, 2013.

36. *Ibid.*

37. Dina Guirguis, "In Response to US Ambassador Anne Patterson," *Atlantic Council*, June 27, 2013, available from *www.atlanticcouncil.org/blogs/egyptsource/in-response-to-us-ambassador-anne-patterson*; see also "Egypt Opposition Group Criticizes 'Blatant Interference' by US Ambassador," *ahramonline*, June 19, 2013.

38. John Lederman, "US Officials Decline to Take Sides in Conflict," *The Boston Globe*, July 5, 2013.

39. David Kirkpatrick, "Egypt's Liberals Embrace the Military, Brooking No Dissent," *The New York Times*, July 18, 2013.

40. Jason Breslow, "Who's Who in Egypt's Widening Political Divide?" *PBS.org*, July 17, 2013, available from *www.pbs.org/wgbh/pages/frontline/foreign-affairs-defense/revolution-in-cairo-foreign-affairs-defense/whos-who-in-egypts-widening-political-divide-2/*.

41. Lally Weymouth, "Harsh Words for US from Egypt," *The Washington Post*, August 2, 2013.

42. Sharanbir Grewal, "The Logic of Partially Suspending Aid to Egypt," *The Washington Post*, October 12, 2013.

43. Amy Hawthorne, "Congress and the Reluctance to Stop US Aid to Egypt," *Atlantic Council*, January 14, 2014, available from *www.atlanticcouncil.org/blogs/egyptsource/congress-and-the-reluctance-to-stop-us-aid-to-egypt*.

44. Phil Stewart and Arshad Mohammed, "US to deliver Apache Helicopters to Egypt, Relaxing Hold on Aid," *Reuters*, April 23, 2014; Ernesto Londono, "U.S. to Partially Resume Military Aid to Egypt," *The Washington Post*, April 23, 2014.

45. Will Dunham, "U.S. Says Imposing Egypt's Death Sentences Would be 'Unconscionable,'" *Reuters*, March 25, 2014.

46. Beaumont.

47. "Foreign Leaders Hail Tunisia's Constitution," *Al Jazeera*, February 7, 2014.

48. "U.S. Secretary of State Visits Tunis, Praises New Constitution," May 12, 2014, available from *www.tunisia-live.net/2014/02/18/u-s-secretary-of-state-visits-tunis-praises-new-constitution/*.

49. *Ibid.*

50. "Obama Praises Tunisia as Model of Arab Spring," *Al-Arabiya News*, April 5, 2014.

51. "Obama Praises Tunisia as Paragon of Arab Spring," *The Jordan Times*, April 5, 2014, available from *www.the-news-page.com/news_details.aspx?ID=17790*.

52. For an interesting analysis on Tunisia, see Shadi Hamid, *Temptations of Power: Islamists and Illiberal Democracy in a New Middle East*, New York: Oxford University Press, 2014, pp. 190-194.

53. While not all Islamist parties are the same and some are more moderate than others, they generally share an antipathy toward U.S. policies in the region. For example, the Brotherhood came out strongly against the Western-supported Gulf War against Iraq in 1991-92 and the Madrid Peace Talks in 1992. See Wickham, pp. 76-77.

54. See Sullivan and Abed-Kotb, pp. 41-42, for the ideology of Hassan Al-Banna, the founder of the Brotherhood. They write that Al-Banna argued that Egypt's Islamic culture and heritage had been supplanted by Western traditions. Egypt should not import foreign political ideals because the Islamic state is more complete, more pure, more lofty, and more exulted than anything that can be found in the utterances of Westerners and the books of Europeans.

55. BBC documentary, "The Other Side of Suez," published on July 22, 2012.

56. "What's New in Egypt's Draft Constitution," BBC News, December 5, 2013, available from *www.bbc.com/news/world-middle-east-25204313*; See also "Inside Egypt's Draft Constitution: Role of Sharia Redefined," *ahramonline*, December 12, 2013.

57. In his Egyptian television interviews in early-May 2014, former Defense Minister and now presidential candidate al-Sissi said that the protest law, enacted in November 2013, was a means of countering "chaos." See Laura King, "Egyptian Presidential Candidate Sisi: Muslim Brotherhood 'Finished'," *The Los Angeles Times*, May 6, 2014.

58. "Secular Leader in Tunisia Says Alliance with En-Nahda Possible," *Middle East Monitor*, March 18, 2014, available from *https://www.middleeastmonitor.com/news/africa/10379-secular-leader-in-tunisia-says-alliance-with-ennahda-possible*.

59. King.

60. Abigail Hauslohner and Erin Cunningham, "Police Station Bombings, Clashes Kill 10 in Egypt," *The Washington Post*, January 25, 2014.

61. Khaled Dawoud, "Point of No Return," *El Tahrir* newspaper, December 28, 2013, available from *arabist.net/blog/2014/1/8/point-of-no-return*.

62. Paul Ginsborg, *A History of Contemporary Italy: Society and Politics, 1943-1988*, New York: Penguin Books, 1990, p. 84.

63. *Ibid.*, p. 85.

64. *Ibid.*, pp. 89-90.

65. *Ibid.*, p. 90.

66. See the article by James E. Miller, "Taking Off the Gloves: The United States and the Italian Election of 1948," *Diplomatic History*, Vol. 20, 1983.

67. Irwin Wall, *The United States and the Making of Postwar France, 1945-1954*, Cambridge, UK: Cambridge University Press, 1991, pp. 50-61.

68. *Ibid.*, and Ginsborg, pp. 95-110.

69. It is likely that any U.S. pronouncements on the role of the *sharia* would be misinterpreted in the highly polarized environment of today's Arab countries. Hence, U.S. policymakers should continue to stay away from this issue.

70. Hamid writes that "Whenever the Brotherhood faced a crisis, its immediate instinct was to call for elections . . ." See his article, "The Future of Democracy in the Middle East," p. 7.

71. In late-December 2011, the Egyptian authorities cracked down on American and European NGOs involved in democracy promotion in Egypt, shut their offices, and confiscated their equipment. This event caused a crisis in U.S.-Egyptian relations for a time. Such NGOs are still prohibited from working in Egypt.

72. "Remarks by the President on the Situation in Egypt," Washington, DC: The White House, Office of the Press Secretary,

August 15, 2013, available from *www.whitehouse.gov/the-press-of-fice/2013/08/15/remarks-president-situation-egypt*.

73. Dunne.

74. "EU representative Ashton in Cairo to Meet with Political Powers," Mada Masr, July 17, 2013 *madamasr.com/content/eu-representative-ashton-cairo-meet-political-powers*.

75. Ambassador Anne W. Patterson's Speech.

76. Some analysts take a different view, such as Amy Hawthorne, "Getting Democracy Promotion Right in Egypt," *Atlantic Council*, Issue Brief, January 2014, pp. 3-4.

77. "What's New in Egypt's Draft Constitution."

78. See al-Sissi's interview with Weymouth, "Harsh Words for US from Egypt."

79. Mohamed Abdu Hassanien, "Egypt Fears 'Ikhwanization' of Military," Asharq Al-Awsat, March 20, 2013, available from *www.aawsat.net/2013/03/article55296303*.

80. One analyst has written, "Not a lot is known about Sisi's private life and inclinations, but he has had a reputation for being a religious man." See Paul R. Pillar, "Intolerance in Sisi's Egypt," *Middle East Eye*, May 8, 2014, available from *www.middleeasteye.net/columns/intolerance-sisis-egypt*.

81. "Sinai Residents Complain of Violations by Egypt Army," *Al-Monitor*, May 7, 2014, available from *www.al-monitor.com/pulse/originals/2014/05/egypt-sinai-war-on-terror-civilians.html*.

U.S. ARMY WAR COLLEGE

Major General William E. Rapp
Commandant

*****

STRATEGIC STUDIES INSTITUTE
and
U.S. ARMY WAR COLLEGE PRESS

Director
Professor Douglas C. Lovelace, Jr.

Director of Research
Dr. Steven K. Metz

Author
Mr. Gregory Aftandilian

Editor for Production
Dr. James G. Pierce

Publications Assistant
Ms. Rita A. Rummel

*****

Composition
Mrs. Jennifer E. Nevil

www.ingramcontent.com/pod-product-compliance
Lightning Source LLC
Chambersburg PA
CBHW071120280526
45787CB00003B/1110